Old Jack's Ghost Stories from Scotland

I Talk You Talk Press

CONTENTS

ACKNOWLEDGMENTS

With sincere thanks to Colin Dixon who collected and recorded the stories contained in this volume. Without his contribution this book would not have been possible.

MESSAGE FROM OLD JACK

Hello my friends! Welcome to my third book of ghost stories. In this book, I travel north of England to the land of the Scots.

Scotland is famous for its beautiful scenery. It has many mountains and lakes. The lakes in Scotland are called 'lochs'. The most famous loch is 'Loch Ness'. People say there is a big monster living in the waters of Loch Ness.

Scotland is also known for its world-famous spirit 'Scotch whisky'. I like this spirit. I often drink it. This book has stories about spirits, but they are not alcohol spirits. No, these spirits are not in a bottle. They are in the castles, hotels and homes of this land. They are the spirits of the dead, who stay on this earth and in this country.

Are you ready to hear about these stories? Let's go to Scotland now. Our first stop is in the very old and beautiful city of Edinburgh.

1. MR BOOTS

Place: Edinburgh Vaults, Edinburgh

Edinburgh is the capital of Scotland. It is also one of the most popular cities in Britain for tourists. Over a million tourists visit the city every year. Most tourists go to Edinburgh Castle and the National Museum of Scotland. They take bus tours around the city. They enjoy taking photographs of the old city streets and beautiful buildings. Then, they go shopping in the city's many shops.

There is one tourist spot in Edinburgh that only the bravest tourists visit. A dark tourist spot deep under the city, with a very sad history. This place is called Edinburgh Vaults. The 'vaults' are tunnels and rooms underground.

In Edinburgh, there is a long bridge called South Bridge. It was built in the 18th century. On the bridge there is a road. Under the bridge, there are many arches and tunnels. The bridge designers decided to make rooms in these arches and tunnels under the bridge.

The tunnels and rooms were very dark. There was no light, no fresh air and no water. At first, shop owners used these rooms. They stored their products in them. Some workmen used them too, but it was very hard to work in these dark rooms under the bridge. So, the workers moved away.

After the workers moved away, the poor people of the city moved into these rooms. Families lived in these dark, damp, smelly rooms. They had no water, no fresh air and no light. The living conditions were very bad. It was also very dangerous to live there. There were many robberies and murders. Many people died. There are many

2

tragic stories from the Edinburgh Vaults.

The conditions in the vaults were very bad, so the city government closed them in the 19th century. No one could go into the Edinburgh Vaults. For a long time, the Edinburgh Vaults were forgotten. Edinburgh grew into a big city, and no one talked about the tunnels and rooms and their dark secrets under the city.

Then, in the 1980s, the Edinburgh Vaults were discovered again when the bridge was being repaired. The tunnels and rooms were made into a tourist attraction.

Would you like to go on a tour of the Edinburgh Vaults? If you do, you must be very brave. There are many ghost stories from the long, dark and sad history of the Edinburgh Vaults.

Last autumn, I was sitting in a hotel bar in Edinburgh enjoying a glass of whisky. Whisky that is made in Scotland is called 'Scotch'. I was reading the local newspaper. Suddenly, an American tourist came running into the bar. I was very surprised. He looked very frightened.

He ran to the bar and said to the barman, "A double whisky please. No ice." The barman looked at the man's hands. The tourist's hands were shaking. The barman asked him, "Are you OK? What's wrong?"

The tourist didn't answer. He sat down on a bar stool. He tried to breathe deeply. He drank all his whisky in a second, and said to the barman, "Another one, please."

The barman poured him another double whisky. He drank that quickly, too.

Then, the tourist said to the barman, "I just took a tour of the Edinburgh Vaults."

"I see," said the barman. "Is it frightening down there, under the city?"

The tourist nodded his head. "Yes, and I...I...there was a man...I..." The tourist couldn't speak.

I put my newspaper down and listened very carefully. The barman also listened carefully.

"What happened? Tell me," said the barman.

"Well," said the tourist. "I was in a tour group. There were around ten of us. It was very dark. When I went down into the vaults, I felt very scared. I didn't like it. I felt like someone was watching me. I was at the back of the tour group.

"The guide took us into a long, dark tunnel. She told us about the

history. She said, 'There were many murders here'. Then...then..."
The tourist stopped.

The barman poured another whisky and gave it to him. Everyone in the pub was quiet. Everyone was listening to the tourist.

"Then what?" asked a man sitting at the bar.

"Then, someone touched my back," said the tourist.

"Who touched your back? Another tour group member?" asked the barman.

The tourist shook his head. "No, no. I was at the back of the group. I turned around, but there was no one there. We continued walking down the tunnel. Then, I heard a voice. The voice was angry. It whispered in my ear, 'Get out! Get out!'

"I shouted to the tour guide. I shouted, 'Stop! Someone is here! Someone said, 'Get out!' Everyone in the group became very quiet. They were very frightened. Then, we heard footsteps. Heavy footsteps, like big boots. A woman in the tour group screamed. She said, 'I want to go out. I don't want to stay here.' So, the guide said, 'Let's go back.'

"We were walking back to the entrance, when something touched me again. I turned around and I saw a shadow! The shadow was behind me!"

"What kind of shadow?" asked the barman.

"The shadow of a man! A big man! With a big hat! Then, I heard a man laughing quietly in my ear!"

"Ah, Mr Boots," said an old man sitting at a table in the corner.

Everyone looked at the old man.

"Pardon?" said the tourist.

"You met Mr Boots," said the old man.

"Mr Boots?"

"Yes, Mr Boots," said the old man. He walked over to the bar and sat on a bar stool next to the tourist. "Mr Boots is the most evil ghost in the vaults. Some people say he did very bad things in the vaults when he was alive. Some people say he was a criminal. Other people say he murdered people."

"Why is he called Mr Boots?" asked the tourist.

"Because he wore big heavy boots," said the old man. "And tourists, like you, sometimes hear his footsteps."

The old man looked at the tourist. "You were lucky," he said.

"Lucky? Why?" asked the tourist.

"Well, Mr Boots doesn't like tourists. He doesn't like people going into his vaults. He said to you, 'Get out!' He touched your back. But sometimes, he hits tourists very hard. Sometimes he pushes them, or pulls their clothes."

The barman nodded. "The story of Mr Boots is famous in Edinburgh," he said.

"I'm never going into the vaults again," said the tourist.

"No, I never go there," said the barman.

I went to the bar and ordered another whisky.

"Have you been to the vaults yet Old Jack?" asked the barman.

"No, not yet," I said.

"Would you like to?" asked the barman.

"After hearing that story, I think I would need to drink a few glasses of Scotch before I went down into those vaults," I said.

2. THE POLTERGEIST

Place: Greyfriars Kirkyard, Old Town, Edinburgh

The history between Scotland and England is a long and often violent one. There were many wars and many people died in battles. For this story, let's stay in Edinburgh and go back to the year 1638. The king of England at that time was Charles I (the first). He wanted everyone in England and Scotland to use a prayer book called the Book of Common Prayer.

Many people in Scotland did not like this. They did not want to use the prayer book. That year, many Scots gathered in a Scottish church called Greyfriars Kirk. 'Kirk' is the Scottish word for 'church'. They signed a Covenant (a kind of law or promise). They said, "We do not want to use the book. We will not use it!"

After that there were twenty-five long years of war. The Scottish lost the war after the Battle at Bothwell Bridge in 1679. Many supporters of the Covenant were arrested and taken to Edinburgh. They became prisoners. Soon the prison became very full, so 400 prisoners were taken to Greyfriars Kirk and kept in the churchyard. The guard who watched these prisoners was George Mackenzie. He was a very cruel and bad man. He gave the prisoners very little food.

As time passed, many prisoners died. Some were killed and some died of illness. England had a new king – he was also called Charles. Some prisoners promised to support the English king Charles II (the second), and so they became free. Soon, only about 250 prisoners were left. They were sent away from Scotland, across the sea. The boat they were in had trouble, and one stormy night it sank. So, the terrible story of the prisoners ended.

Today, the prisoners' area of Greyfriars Kirkyard is called The Covenanters' Prison.

What happened to George Mackenzie? Well, he died in 1691 and was buried in a fine tomb in the churchyard.

Next to the churchyard, there is an old pub. The pub's name is Greyfriars Bobby. It is an interesting name, isn't it? There is an interesting story about this pub's name.

Bobby was a small dog. His owner died and was buried in the churchyard. Bobby refused to leave his owner's grave. Bobby stayed in the churchyard, guarding his owner's grave until he died. So, this pub was named after this loyal dog.

I met John, an old friend, in this pub. It was a cold, autumn afternoon. The sky outside was dark and it was very windy.

John said to me, "Old Jack, you write books about ghost stories, don't you?"

"Yes, I do," I said.

"Well," said John, "I'm going to tell you a terrible story. You can put this story in your book of ghost stories."

I opened my notebook, picked up my pen, and listened to John's story.

He said, "One cold winter's night in 1999, there was a homeless man. He was looking for somewhere to sleep. He came into the churchyard and found Mackenzie's tomb. The homeless man had an idea. He thought, 'The tomb is big. I can sleep in there'. So, he broke into the tomb. When he was breaking into the tomb, a man walking his dog heard the noise. The man called the police and the homeless man ran away. Since that time, many strange things have happened in this churchyard."

"Strange things?" I asked. "What kind of strange things?"

"Well, since December 1999, hundreds of people have been attacked in the churchyard."

"Attacked? By whom?" I asked.

"By an invisible spirit. Many people who were attacked had blood and scratches on their legs, arms and backs. Some people had bruises on their bodies. Some were pushed to the ground. They hit their heads on the ground and were unconscious."

"That's terrible," I said. "Can you take me to the place?"

John laughed. "Old Jack, you are not young anymore. Do you

really want to go there?"

"Oh yes," I said. "I'm not too old for an adventure."

John laughed. "OK. Let's go and take a look," he said.

We put our coats on and walked out of the pub. It was early evening now, and the sky was growing dark. We arrived at the area near Mackenzie's tomb, but there was a gate, with a very big lock.

"Why can't we enter?" I asked my friend.

"Because it is not safe," said my friend. "So many people were attacked. It is a very dangerous place. The city government locked it."

"So we can't go in?"

"No, we can't. But there is a special tour for tourists. Tourist groups can go in, but only with a special guide. It is too dangerous to go alone."

I looked through the gates at the churchyard in the dark early evening. The shadows were long, and the wind in the trees was noisy. I shivered. I was glad to turn away and go back to the warm pub, and another glass of Scotch.

Later that night, in my hotel room, I thought about the story. I think it is unusual. Ghosts usually do not stay in churchyards. They prefer to visit places where they spent time when they were alive. Many people think the attacker is the ghost of George Mackenzie. He is very angry because the homeless man broke into his tomb. Now, when he sees people near his tomb, he attacks them.

It was my last night in Edinburgh. I had no time to take the special tour of the Greyfriars Kirkyard. *Maybe next time,* I thought. If you go to Edinburgh, will you take the tour? If you do, be very careful…

3. THE RED ROOM

Place: Borthwick Castle, North Middleton, Midlothian

After I left Edinburgh last autumn, I travelled a few miles south through the beautiful Midlothian countryside. I enjoyed walking through the hills and farmlands. The leaves on the trees were changing colour, from green to autumn red and orange. It was a beautiful time of year.

I stayed in a small guesthouse for a few days. The owner was very friendly, and one night we sat in the bar until late, drinking Scotch and talking.

"Where are you going tomorrow?" he asked.

"Borthwick Castle," I said.

"Ah, Borthwick Castle. Yes, it is very near here. Do you know anything about the castle?"

"Well, I know that it is used for weddings and other events," I said. "And it's very old. It was built in the 15th century. Mary, Queen of Scots stayed there."

"Yes, that's right. She hid in the castle. Some people were looking for her. They wanted to arrest her."

"Did the people find her in the castle?"

"No, she escaped. She put on men's clothes, so she looked like a man. Then, she jumped through a window and escaped. When you go to the castle, you can see the window. And, you might see Mary."

"Pardon? How can I see Mary? She died in the 15th century!" I said.

"Well, some people have seen a woman dressed in very old-

9

fashioned men's clothes. People say the woman is the ghost of Mary, Queen of Scots."

"Really?" I asked.

"Oh yes. Her ghost still walks the castle stairs."

I smiled. "I'm looking forward to going to the castle. Thank you for telling me that story."

"Oh, there are many more stories too," said the guesthouse owner. "Do you know about the red room?"

"The red room?" I asked. "What's that?"

"Well, long ago, there was a poor young girl. She became pregnant by the Lord of Borthwick Castle. Of course, this was terrible news for the lord. So he locked her in one of the castle bedrooms. He was worried that the child might try to become lord in the future. That would cause many problems for the lord's family.

"So, he did something terrible. He told his soldiers to go to the room and kill the girl and her child.

"People said that when the girl and her child died, the walls of the room became red with their blood. After that, no one used the room again."

"That's a terrible story," I said.

"Oh, I haven't finished," said the guesthouse owner. "The castle became a hotel in 1973. The owners decided to use the red room. To keep the story alive, they painted the walls red and bought red curtains and bed sheets. All the room was red. The room became a guest room."

"That's an interesting idea," I said. "Do many people stay in the room?"

"Oh yes. Many people have stayed in the room, and many people have had strange experiences."

"What kind of strange experiences?" I asked.

"Well, this is interesting. A few months ago, a woman stayed here in my guesthouse. We were talking about Borthwick Castle. She stayed there a few years ago. She stayed in the Red Room. She told me this story.

"She woke up in the middle of the night. She could hear footsteps outside the room. Then, the room suddenly became very cold. She could hear a very quiet voice. She said it was like the voice of a young girl. She thought, 'It must be a hotel worker. But why are they still walking around at this time?' She went back to sleep, but very soon,

10

she was woken up again. This time, she knew it was not a hotel worker. She switched the light on, and she saw a young girl sitting on the chair. The young girl looked very sad. The woman thought the girl was crying. Suddenly, the girl disappeared. Then she heard strange noises in the walls. She didn't go back to sleep that night. She was too frightened. She stayed awake all night with the light on."

"Who was the girl?" I asked.

"I think it was the ghost of the young girl," said the guesthouse owner. "People say she comes back to the room. She is crying because her baby was killed."

"That's a very sad story," I said. "Has anyone else seen her?"

"Oh yes. Many people have seen and heard her," said the guesthouse owner. "If you go there tomorrow, you might see her too."

I took a long drink of my whisky and decided not to go to the Red Room on my visit to Borthwick Castle.

4. THE INJURED SPIRIT

Place: Leith Hall, Huntly, Aberdeen and Grampian

We travel north now, to the beautiful land of Aberdeenshire. Here we find Leith Hall. The hall was built in 1650 by the Leith Family. It was kept in the family until 1945, when it was given to the National Trust of Scotland. If you visit Aberdeen, I recommend you visit Leith Hall. It is in the middle of beautiful countryside and has wonderful gardens. It is a very nice place to spend a summer afternoon.

However, Leith Hall hides a dark secret. Let's go back to a few days before Christmas in 1763.

The lord of the hall, John Leith, was in a pub. He was drunk and he was having a fight with another man about something. The other man was also drunk. No one knows what they were fighting about, but they were very angry with each other. The other drinkers in the pub were watching the fight. Then, they heard a shot. John fell to the floor. His head was bleeding. He had been shot. A few days later, on Christmas Day, he died.

John's family said, "He was murdered! The other man killed him!"

There were many people drinking in the pub at the time, but they said, "I didn't see anything." No one talked about it. John's family believed that the man killed John, but the man said, "No, I was protecting myself. He tried to kill me!"

Let's come forward to the 1960s, when the writer Elizabeth Byrd was staying in Leith Hall with her family. She stayed there for a few years. During that time, she experienced strange events. Doors closed by themselves, and there were strange sounds coming from empty rooms. Sometimes her friends came to visit her. They didn't like Leith Hall. In particular, they didn't like the master bedroom on the second floor.

One night, Elizabeth and her husband went to bed. During the night, she woke up. It was very dark in the room.

What's that? she thought. She could hear a man's voice in the centre of the room.

Who is that? Who is in our room? she thought. She switched a small lamp on. In the shadows, she saw a man. There was blood on the man's face. He had a bandage wrapped around his head. He didn't look like a ghost. He looked like a real man.

She sat up in bed and pointed to the door. Very strongly, she said, "Go!" The man walked towards the bed. He was looking at her, and he was walking towards her. She said in a much stronger voice, "Go now!"

The man looked at her. Then, he turned and walked away. He disappeared into a wall. After that night, the writer's dog would not go into the room. He stood at the door to the room and growled. I think dogs are very sensitive. I think they can feel ghosts.

Who was that man? I think it was the ghost of John Leith. Maybe he wanted to tell the writer about that night so many years ago in the pub. Maybe he wanted to tell her the truth. Maybe he wanted her to write about it. We will never know the reason.

The ghost of John is not the only ghost in Leith Hall. There are many more. Some visitors have heard footsteps. Some people have heard a woman laughing or seen the ghosts of children playing in bedrooms.

If you go to Leith Hall, I hope you enjoy your visit. I recommend you go in summer, when there are many visitors and a lot of sunlight. If you go, I hope you don't see a man with blood and a bandage on his head. If you do see him, and he starts to walk towards you, remember this story. Be strong. Tell him to go away!

5. THE DREAMING GUEST

Place: Tulloch Castle, Dingwall, Ross-Shire

Now we travel north of Aberdeen, all the way to the wonderful highlands of Scotland. Here, in the far north of Scotland there is a small town called Dingwall. This town has a very old castle. Tulloch Castle was built in the 12th century. Of course, the building has changed many times since then. Long ago, it was the home of the Davidson family. Today, it is a luxury hotel.

Now, Tulloch Castle is peaceful and relaxing, but its long and sometimes dark history still echoes around its old walls.

The castle has many ghost stories, but I think this next story is the best.

A few years ago, a businessman from Edinburgh was staying at the hotel. He stayed in Room 8. Many people have had strange experiences in this room.

One night, he woke up. The room temperature was changing. It was very hot, and then suddenly it became very cold. Then it was hot again, and then it was cold again. He tried to go to sleep again, but he couldn't. He felt pressure on his chest. It was like someone was sitting on him.

After a few hours, he fell asleep. While he was sleeping, he had a dream. In his dream, he was back at home in Edinburgh. The doorbell rang.

Who is that? he thought. *I'm not expecting any visitors.*

He went to the door and opened it. He was very surprised. There were two little girls aged around six or seven. They were wearing old-fashioned clothes. They were standing in front of his house and they were looking at him. At the gate of his house, there was a middle-aged lady. She looked very strict. She was looking at him.

Suddenly the man woke up. He was sweating and shaking.

What was that? That was a really strange dream, he thought. *Who were those girls? Who was that woman?* After a few minutes, he fell asleep again.

In the morning, he went downstairs to breakfast. He told the manager about his strange dream.

The manager asked him, "Have you seen the Great Hall yet?"

"No, I haven't," said the man.

"Follow me," said the manager.

They walked into the Great Hall.

"I don't believe it!" said the man.

On the wall there was a painting of a family. In the painting, there were two little girls aged around six or seven. They were wearing old-fashioned clothes.

"They are the same girls!" said the man. "I saw them in my dream! They are wearing the same clothes! They have the same faces!"

"I'll switch the lights on so you can see better," said the manager.

The manager switched the lights on and BANG! All the lights in the hall broke at the same time. It was very dark. But there were two lights which did not break. These lights were the two lights above the painting.

The manager and the man looked around the hall. The manager tried to turn the lights on, but the lights were broken. They quickly walked out of the Great Hall.

Later, the lighting system in the hall was checked. The light repairman could not find any problems with the lights. They were working fine.

Why did the lights suddenly break? I think the manager should ask the girls in the painting. I think the girls know the answer. I think they were playing games with the businessman and the manager. Or maybe they wanted to tell the businessman something. Maybe they wanted to communicate with him. No one knows…

6. THE BATHROOM

Place: Blythswood Square, Glasgow

We cannot leave Scotland without a visit to its largest city, Glasgow.

Glasgow is an exciting city. If you visit Glasgow as a tourist, you will probably go to the West End area. There are many hotels, shops, cafes and bars in this area. The University of Glasgow is here too, so there are many young people, academics and artists. I like walking around this area of Glasgow and sitting in its cafes. You can hear many stories when you sit in cafes.

This is a story I heard in a café in the West End. I was enjoying a cup of coffee. At the next table there were two women. One woman was Scottish. The other woman was French. The Scottish woman was telling the French woman a story. The story sounded interesting, so I listened very carefully. It was a story about Blythswood Square.

When the woman finished telling the story, I looked at the map in my guidebook. I was happy to see that the square was only a thirty minute walk from the West End. I finished my coffee and hurried across the West End, past the university, to Blythswood Square.

This square was built around 1830. Around the square are pretty townhouses. When they were built, they were very expensive, and rich businessmen and their families lived there.

In the 19th century, a rich businessman's family went to look at one of the townhouses. They planned to rent it. They were happy with the house. It was large and in the city centre. It was very convenient.

16

There was only one problem. When they were looking around the house, the man of the family did not like the bathroom. It had a small window and a drying cupboard with a large door. He felt something strange in the bathroom.

The family decided to rent the house, but before they moved into the house, the man had the bathroom re-painted and re-fitted. He wanted to make the bathroom brighter and more cheerful.

One evening, the man of the family went to the bathroom to have a bath. He filled the bath with water and started to take his clothes off. Suddenly the candle went out! It was completely dark.

What's happening? he thought. He looked for the candle, but he fell over because it was dark. He tried to stand up. Then, he heard the sound of someone washing in the bath.

Who is that? he thought. *Who is in the bath?*

Then, the drying cupboard door opened slowly. A smell of violets, like perfume, filled the air. He felt a long skirt touch his face. Then, he felt a woman stand on him! She was trying to walk to the bath.

The man was so frightened that he could not speak or move. He heard the sound of a fight in the water and someone in the bath shouted. He looked up and in the darkness, he saw the white face of a woman. The face was glowing very brightly. She was smiling, but it was not a happy smile. It was an evil smile. She turned away from him and walked back into the drying cupboard.

The man was very frightened. He ran out of the bathroom. He ran to the living room. He said to his wife and children, "Quick! Come to the bathroom! There's a woman in the bathroom!"

They all ran to the bathroom. They opened the door. The room was very calm and peaceful. There was no woman in the bathroom. The man's wife was not happy.

"There is no woman here! You are dreaming. You are dreaming about a woman!" she said.

For a few days, everything in the house was normal. Then, one morning, the son of the family went to the bathroom. He looked in the bath and screamed. There was the body of a dead man in the bath! His family heard his screams. They all ran to the bathroom, but they couldn't see anything.

Then, a dark-haired woman appeared. They all saw her. She had very evil eyes. She walked past them and disappeared into the drying cupboard.

The family soon left the house. They didn't want to live there anymore. Later, they heard that the first owner of the house was a rich man. He married a very young woman. The woman was young enough to be his grand-daughter. One day, she said to people, "I found my husband. He was dead in the bath. I think he fainted and drowned."

After that, she got all his money and then she left Scotland. Did the rich man really faint and drown? Or did the young girl kill her rich husband? Did she kill him because she wanted his money? Did the family who rented the house see and hear the real story? Did they see the girl murder her husband?

We will never know.

I walked slowly around the square. I wondered which building the story was about. The woman in the café telling the story said, "It's a secret. No one knows which building the story is about." I looked at the luxury hotel, houses and office buildings. *It doesn't look like a place where evil lives,* I thought. *Or maybe, the square is good at hiding its dark history…*

THANK YOU

Thank you for reading Old Jack's Ghost Stories from Scotland. (Word count: 5,188) Old Jack hopes you enjoyed reading his stories.

For more information about the places in this book, please visit http://www.italk-youtalk.com. There is a page with maps and photographs of the places that Old Jack has written about.

If you would like to read more graded readers, please visit our website http://www.italkyoutalk.com

Other graded readers by Old Jack:
Old Jack's Ghost Stories from England (1)
Old Jack's Ghost Stories from England (2)
Old Jack's Ghost Stories from Wales
Old Jack's Ghost Stories from Ireland
Old Jack's Ghost Stories from Japan

NOTES AND REFERENCES

1. Mr Boots
Edinburgh Vaults, 28 South Bridge, Edinburgh EH1 1LL
The story is based on information found on the following sites:
http://en.wikipedia.org/wiki/Edinburgh_Vaults
(Retrieved August 2013)
http://www.scotsman.com/news/sounds-like-vaults-are-haunted-after-all-1-866544
(Retrieved August 2013)
http://www.spookystuff.co.uk/aguidetoghostlyedinburgh.html
(Retrieved August 2013)

2. The Poltergeist
Greyfriars Kirkyard, Edinburgh, City of Edinburgh
The story is based on information found on the following sites
http://www.infoplease.com/encyclopedia/society/covenanters.html
(Retrieved August 2013)
http://en.wikipedia.org/wiki/Battle_of_Bothwell_Bridge
(Retrieved August 2013)
http://www.scotsman.com/news/moat-haunted-1-1142541
(Retrieved August 2013)

3. The Red Room
Borthwick Castle, North Middleton, Midlothian EH23 4QY, United Kingdom

http://borthwickcastle.com/
The story is based on information found on the following sites:
http://haunted-scotland.co.uk/borthwick-castle/
(Retrieved August 2013)
http://caledonianmercury.com/2010/03/23/13-haunted-scottish-castles/003988 (Retrieved August 2013)
http://ezinearticles.com/?The-Ghost-of-Mary,-Queen-of-Scots-and-Other-Hauntings-at-Borthwick-Castle&id=7821054
(Retrieved August 2013)

4. The Injured Spirit
Leith Hall Garden & Estate, Huntly, Aberdeen & Grampian AB54 4NQ
http://www.nts.org.uk/Property/Leith-Hall-Garden-Estate/
The story is based on information found on the following sites:
http://en.wikipedia.org/wiki/Leith_Hall#cite_note-aa-3
(Retrieved August 2013)
http://www.aboutaberdeen.com/leithhallghosts.php
(Retrieved August 2013)
http://www.dailyrecord.co.uk/news/scottish-news/haunted-house-leith-hall-reveals-2151550
(Retrieved August 2013)

5. The Dreaming Guest
Tulloch Castle, Tulloch Castle Dr, Dingwall, Ross-Shire IV15 9ND
http://www.bespokehotels.com/tullochcastlehotel/
The story is based on information found on the following sites:
http://en.wikipedia.org/wiki/Tulloch_Castle
(Retrieved August 2013)
The story about the businessman is based on the story of Tommy Tan, originally told in The Ross-Shire Journal, 30 January, 2004, and written on the following sites:
http://ghosts-uk.net/modules/news/article.php?storyid=381
(Retrieved August 2013)
http://haunted-scotland.co.uk/tulloch-castle/
(Retrieved August 2013)

6. The Bathroom

Blythswood Square, Blythswood Hill, Glasgow

The story is based on information found in the following book and on the following site:

O Donnell, Elliot. Scottish Ghost Stories First published in 1912. (The edition used: 2011, The Floating Press) From page 84

http://books.google.co.jp/books?id=TpBHDaovLEsC&printsec=frontcover&hl=ja#v=onepage&q&f=false

(Retrieved August 2013)

http://www.scotsman.com/news/ghosts-in-the-bathroom-scotland-s-real-life-moaning-myrtle-1-465766

(Retrieved August 2013)

ABOUT THE AUTHOR

I Talk You Talk Press is a Japan-based publisher of language textbooks, graded readers and language learning/teaching resources.

Our team is made up of highly experienced language teachers and translators, who have all studied at least one additional language to an advanced level.

This experience enables us to design our materials from the perspective of both the teacher and the learner. We consult with both teachers and language learners when designing our textbooks and graded readers, and test our materials extensively in the classroom before publication.

We are a fast-growing press, and currently publish graded readers for learners of English. We publish new graded readers monthly.

www.ingramcontent.com/pod-product-compliance
Lightning Source LLC
Chambersburg PA
CBHW022352040426
42449CB00006B/839